ASTON VILLA
FOOTBALL CLUB

The Official Annual 2020

Compiled by Rob Bishop and ArenaOne

Special thanks to Gayner Monkton

A Grange Publication

© 2019. Published by Grange Communications Ltd., Edinburgh, under licence from Aston Villa Football Club. Printed in the EU.

Photographs © Neville Williams / Getty Images

ISBN: 978-1-913034-12-2

CLUB HONOURS

EUROPEAN CUP WINNERS:
1981-82

QUARTER-FINALISTS:
1982-83

EUROPEAN SUPER CUP WINNERS:
1982-83

WORLD CLUBS CHAMPIONSHIP RUNNERS-UP:
1982

INTERTOTO CUP WINNERS:
2001

FOOTBALL LEAGUE CHAMPIONS:
1893-94, 1895-96, 1896-97, 1898-99, 1899-1900, 1909-10, 1980-81

RUNNERS-UP:
1888-89, 1902-03, 1907-08, 1910-11, 1912-13, 1913-14, 1930-31, 1932-33, 1989-90

PREMIER LEAGUE RUNNERS-UP:
1992-93

DIVISION TWO CHAMPIONS:
1937-38, 1959-60

DIVISION THREE CHAMPIONS:
1971-72

FA CUP WINNERS:
1887, 1895, 1897, 1905, 1913, 1920, 1957

RUNNERS-UP:
1892, 1924, 2000, 2015

LEAGUE CUP WINNERS:
1961, 1975, 1977, 1994, 1996

RUNNERS-UP:
1963, 1971, 2010

FA YOUTH CUP WINNERS:
1972, 1980, 2002

RUNNERS-UP:
2004, 2010

THE NEW BOYS

Bjorn the jet-setter...

Bjorn Engels is a truly international footballer. He has played in Belgium as well as Greece and France. And he flew to the United States to begin a new career in England!

By the age of 24, the central defender had played for Club Brugge in his home country before joining Greek giants Olympiacos and then French side Stade Reims.

A couple of months before his 25th birthday, he was on the move again. Villa had already flown out to America when the club reached agreement with Reims for his transfer, so he jetted across the Atlantic to undergo his medical before joining his new team-mates at their pre-season training camp in Minnesota.

"Everything was done very quickly," he said. "But it was very exciting to go out to Minnesota to complete the signing.

"I have played in different countries but you can't really compare the Premier League with those countries. The level in England is much higher."

The new boy at school!

You know the feeling you get when you start school, or move to a new one? Well, that's exactly how Matt Targett felt when he joined Villa!

The young full-back signed from Southampton just before Dean Smith's players reported back for pre-season training.

"I was very excited to meet everyone," he said. "It was like being a new boy at school. It's good to develop new friendships, on and off the pitch."

Targett had been part of Southampton's academy from the age of eight. He made his debut for the first team in August 2014, and he was named Southampton's young player of the year for 2014-15.

Apart from 63 appearances for the Saints, he was also partly responsible for Villa not being promoted in 2018. He had a spell on loan to Fulham – and played against us in the play-off final at Wembley!

Captain's orders!

Egypt international Trezeguet revealed that his fellow countryman Ahmed Elmohamady had a big influence on his decision to join Villa from Turkish club Kasimpasa.

"Ahmed is a good friend and is like my brother," he said. "He is my captain for the national team, and he has told me a lot about Aston Villa.

"He said it was an amazing club, and I will do everything I can to make the fans happy. This club has everything you need to be successful."

The winger's real name is Mahmoud Ahmed Ibrahim Hassan, but he has been known as Trezeguet since the age of nine because his playing style is like that of former French star David Trezeguet.

The waiting game...

Football clubs must sometimes be patient when signing a new player. When Villa wanted to sign Frederic Guilbert in January 2019, his French club SM Caen agreed – provided it didn't happen until July.

The outcome was that Guilbert signed for a mid-table Championship club but ended up as a member of a Premier League squad!

Immediately after joining Villa, the French full-back was loaned back to Caen to help them try to avoid relegation from Ligue 1.

It didn't work out, and they went down, but in the meantime Villa were earning promotion, which means Guilbert is now continuing his career as a top-flight footballer.

Head coach Dean Smith believes the hard tackling right-back can enhance his reputation in the world's top league.

"Our French scout picked up on him as one of the hottest properties in the French league," said Smith. "He has a lot of potential and is a welcome addition to the squad."

Just the (return) ticket!

Two of Villa's new signings needed no introduction to their team-mates at the start of the season. They had already spent six months with the club!

Defenders Tyrone Mings and Kortney Hause had arrived on loan in January from Bournemouth and Wolves respectively, and both had played their part in helping Villa to promotion. So it was little wonder that head coach Dean Smith wanted them as part of his squad for the Premier League.

Hause's transfer was quickly concluded, and Mings returned just after the players began their pre-season training schedule.

Mings's reputation with Villa supporters had soared when he was photographed at Bournemouth station after the play-off final, still wearing his Wembley kit.

To launch his permanent signing, Villa posted a video of him at Witton station – unveiling this season's kit!

"It was a nice idea," he said. "It was fitting after I was pictured at Bournemouth with my kit on.

"After last season, it felt a good fit to come back as a permanent player. Wembley was the greatest achievement of my career. Everything that happened led to that day.

"To go to Wembley and win is something you grow up dreaming about. It will stay with me forever."

Tom's new challenge

Most of Villa's summer signings were young players aiming to make a name for themselves in the world's top league.

But when it came to bringing in a new goalkeeper, Dean Smith knew he needed experience. That's why the head coach opted for Tom Heaton, the much-travelled keeper who had played over 100 top-flight games for Burnley.

"The transfer had been on the cards for a while and I was delighted to join a fantastic club who are back in the Premier League," said Heaton.

"This is a new challenge for me. It's a really exciting time for Villa and I'm delighted to be part of that."

Heaton, capped three times by England before his move to Villa Park, started his career at Manchester United but was unable to break into the first team. After leaving Old Trafford, he played for Swindon Town and Bristol City before joining Burnley in 2013.

A red 'hot' signing!

Just imagine if you were called Jose Ignacio Peleteiro Ramallo. Quite a mouthful, isn't it?

But Villa's first signing during the summer transfer window has the perfect solution. He is known as Jota – pronounced "hotter" in his native Spanish – and he is aiming to be too hot to handle for opposition defences!

Like many overseas players with lengthy names, the attacking midfielder uses the nickname to make life easier, both for himself and for supporters.

Jota became the first player to join Villa from our

Second City rivals since Alan Curbishley – and that transfer was 36 years ago.

Born in Spain's Galicia region, Jota began his career with his local club Celta Vigo before moving to England in 2014, when he joined Brentford.

His transfer to Villa means he is reunited with Dean Smith, who was his manager at Griffin Park for two years before his move to Birmingham.

Two promotions in a row!

Sometimes we hear about teams who are promoted in consecutive seasons. Ezri Konsa can make the same claim as a player – even though neither of his clubs went up!

At the end of the 2017-18 campaign, Konsa was a League One player with Charlton Athletic before moving into the Championship by signing for Brentford.

And the following summer he stepped up again, joining a Premier League club when Dean Smith signed him for a second time to bring him to Villa Park.

"As a kid, I always used to dream about playing in the Premier League," said the young central defender. "For it to come true is a fantastic feeling."

Konsa is hoping to spend much longer with Smith and coach Richard O'Kelly than he did at Griffin Park. He signed for Brentford in June 2018, and by October the management duo had taken over at Villa.

"We had a really good relationship at Brentford," he said. "To be working with those guys again is a good feeling."

The Brazilian blend!

Villa had never signed a Brazilian player until this summer – and then two came along within the space of a few weeks!

First up was striker Wesley Moraes, who became the club's record signing when he arrived from Club Brugge of Belgium.

And later in July, central midfielder Douglas Luiz was snapped up from Manchester City.

For Wesley, coming to Villa is a case of living the dream. As a boy, he played against Premier League teams in video games – now he can do it for real!

"It's a real pleasure for me to play against the big teams," he said. "But most of all I want to help Aston Villa to win trophies."

Known simply by his first name, Wesley is delighted that his family will now see far more of him in action, thanks to worldwide broadcasts of English top-flight games.

"When my mum knew I was going to be playing in England she was so happy, just like the rest of my family," he said. "Now it's going to be much easier for them to watch my matches."

Douglas, meanwhile, has been a Man City player for the past two years, and spent last season on loan to Spanish club Girona.

"This is another stage in my career," he said. "I don't speak a lot of English but I hope I can help by shouting orders from the back."

He arrived at Villa Park on a high note after helping Brazil U23s to win the prestigious Toulon Tournament and being voted player of the tournament.

A marvellous player!

His answer may have sounded a touch conceited, but it could not have been more accurate.

Asked to describe himself as a footballer, he replied with a huge grin: "I'm a marvellous player!"

His name is unusual, but Marvelous Nakamba is clearly determined to live up to it following his move from Club Brugge.

The Zimbabwean midfielder makes no secret of his delight in following in the footsteps of striker Wesley to become the second Villa player signed from the Belgian club during the summer transfer window.

"For me to be here is fantastic," he said. "It has always been an ambition of mine to join a Premier League club and I'm looking forward to playing against the best players in the world.

"Wesley told me many good things about Aston Villa, and it's good to have a familiar face in the dressing room. I'm happy to be part of the Villa family."

FREDERIC GUILBERT

AUTOGRAPH

JUST
FANTASTIC

Villa may not have finished top of the table – but they were by far the best-supported team in the Championship last season.

The average attendance for league matches at Villa Park was 36,029 – nearly 2,000 higher than Leeds United, whose average of 34,033 was the second highest in the division.

And that wasn't all. Villa's figure was better than 11 Premier League clubs and was higher than many clubs across Europe. Only seven Spanish, five Italian and three French clubs boasted higher average attendances than those at Villa Park.

The club's biggest league crowd was 41,696 for the visit of champions Norwich City on the final day of the regular season, while the turnstiles also clicked to the tune of over 41,000 in the games against Swansea City, Birmingham City, Leeds and Bristol City.

THAT'S WHAT WE CALL FAN-TASTIC SUPPORT!

BACKGROUND ON THE
BOSS

Dean was born in West Bromwich on 19th March 1971 and although his birthplace was nearer to The Hawthorns than Villa Park, he grew up a Villa supporter.

He began his playing career with Walsall in 1988, although it wasn't the best of times for the Saddlers, who were relegated from the old Second Division to the Fourth Division in consecutive seasons. They were still in the fourth tier by the time he was transferred to Hereford United in the

summer of 1994 for a fee of £80,000 – a club record for the Bulls.

Next stop was Leyton Orient, where Smith was a regular for six seasons and scored 37 goals before stepping up to the second tier with Sheffield Wednesday in 2002. By the time he retired in January 2005, following a brief spell with Port Vale, he had played a total of 677 league and cup games, scoring 67 goals.

In January 2011 he landed his first managerial post when he took over as

Walsall boss. When he was appointed, the Saddlers were nine points adrift at the bottom of League One but he inspired an amazing recovery which saw his team avoid the drop.

After nearly five years in charge at Bescot, he was appointed manager of Brentford in November 2015, and despite working on a limited budget he transformed the London club into one of the most attractive teams in the Championship.

During his time at Griffin Park, the Bees faced Villa five times, winning twice at home and drawing on all three of their visits to Villa Park. No wonder he was the leading contender for the Villa job!

JACK
GREALISH

AUTOGRAPH

DO YOU KNOW? JACK GREALISH

All Villa supporters love Jack Grealish, but just how well do you know our midfield maestro? See if you can answer these questions about one of the most exciting young talents in English football...

1. Against which club did Jack make his debut in a Premier League match in May 2014?

2. His first goal for the club was in September 2015. Who were Villa's opponents that day?

3. Jack is an England under-21 international, but he also played for another country at youth level. Which one?

4. How many times has Jack played for Villa at Wembley?

5. Who were Villa's opponents in his first match as captain?

6. Which team did Jack support as a boy?

Answers on Page 60

THE FIRST GOALS CLUB

TOMMY ELPHICK

HULL CITY (A) 3-1

Timing his run to perfection, Tommy meets Jack Grealish's corner to guide home a header for the equaliser after Hull had taken an early lead.

ANWAR EL GHAZI

SHEFFIELD UTD (A) 1-4

The Egyptian midfielder's low shot on the turn is well-taken but is merely a consolation in a heavy defeat at Bramall Lane.

TAMMY ABRAHAM

ROTHERHAM UTD (H) 2-0

Timing his run perfectly, the young striker calmly strokes the ball into the far corner of the net following Jonathan Kodjia's clever flick.

AHMED ELMOHAMADY

HULL CITY (A) 3-1

Moving on to Conor Hourihane's fine through ball, Elmo fires a low angled drive into the far corner to put Villa ahead.

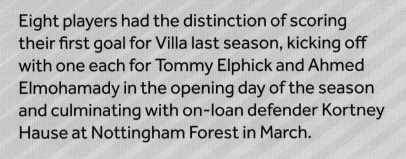

Eight players had the distinction of scoring their first goal for Villa last season, kicking off with one each for Tommy Elphick and Ahmed Elmohamady in the opening day of the season and culminating with on-loan defender Kortney Hause at Nottingham Forest in March.

JOHN McGINN

SHEFFIELD WED. (H) 1-2

The Scottish midfielder's superb 25-yard volley with the outside of his left foot flies in off the underside of the bar for one of the most spectacular goals ever seen at Villa Park.

YANNICK BOLASIE

ROTHERHAM UTD (H) 2-0

Just nine minutes after going on as a sub, Bolasie lunges bravely to score with a diving header from Ahmen Elmohamady's right-wing cross.

TYRONE MINGS

SHEFFIELD UTD (H) 3-3

In only his second Villa game, the on-loan Bournemouth defender climbs in front of keeper Dean Henderson to head home Conor Hourihane's inswinging corner. The goal sparks an amazing late comeback after Villa had been 3-0 down.

KORTNEY HAUSE

NOTTM. FOREST (A) 3-1

With Villa leading 2-1 through two fine John McGinn shots, the on-loan Wolves defender clinches all three points by converting Conor Hourihane's superb free-kick with his chest.

2019|20 SQUAD

Tom Heaton
Goalkeeper

D.O.B.
15.04.86

Birthplace
Chester

Previous Club
Burnley

Date Signed
August 2019

Orjan Nyland
Goalkeeper

D.O.B.
10.09.90

Birthplace
Volda, Norway

Previous Club
Ingolstadt

Date Signed
August 2018

Lovre Kalinic
Goalkeeper

D.O.B.
03.04.90

Birthplace
Split, Croatia

Previous Club
Gent

Date Signed
January 2019

Jed Steer
Goalkeeper

D.O.B.
23.09.92

Birthplace
Norwich

Previous Club
Norwich City

Date Signed
July 2013

Neil Taylor
Defender

D.O.B.
07.02.89

Birthplace
St. Asaph, Wales

Previous Club
Swansea City

Date Signed
January 2017

Tyrone Mings
Defender

D.O.B.
13.03.93

Birthplace
Bath

Previous Club
Bournemouth

Date Signed
July 2019

Bjorn Engels
Defender

D.O.B.
15.09.94

Birthplace
Kaprijke, Belgium

Previous Club
Reims

Date Signed
July 2019

Ezri Konsa
Defender

D.O.B.
23.10.97

Birthplace
Newham

Previous Club
Brentford

Date Signed
July 2019

James Chester
Defender

D.O.B.
23.01.89

Birthplace
Warrington

Previous Club
West Brom

Date Signed
August 2016

Kortney Hause
Defender

D.O.B.
16.07.95

Birthplace
Goodmayes

Previous Club
Wolves

Date Signed
June 2019

19

Frederic Guilbert

Defender

D.O.B.
24.12.94

Birthplace
Valognes, France

Previous Club
Caen

Date Signed
January 2019

Matt Targett

Defender

D.O.B.
18.09.95

Birthplace
Eastleigh

Previous Club
Southampton

Date Signed
June 2019

Conor Hourihane

Midfielder

D.O.B.
02.02.91

Birthplace
Bandon, Ireland

Previous Club
Barnsley

Date Signed
January 2017

Anwar El Ghazi

Midfielder

D.O.B.
03.05.95

Birthplace
Barendrecht, Netherlands

Previous Club
Lille OSC

Date Signed
August 2018

Douglas Luiz
Midfielder

D.O.B.
09.05.98

Birthplace
Rio de Janeiro, Brazil

Previous Club
Manchester City

Date Signed
July 2019

Ahmed Elmohamady
Midfielder

D.O.B.
09.09.87

Birthplace
Basyoun, Egypt

Previous Club
Hull City

Date Signed
July 2017

Marvelous Nakamba
Midfielder

D.O.B.
19.01.94

Birthplace
Hwange, Zimbabwe

Previous Club
Club Brugge

Date Signed
August 2019

Jack Grealish
Midfielder

D.O.B.
10.09.95

Birthplace
Birmingham

Previous Club
N/A

Date Signed
Academy Graduate

Henri Lansbury
Midfielder

D.O.B.
12.10.90

Birthplace
London

Previous Club
Nottingham Forest

Date Signed
January 2017

John McGinn
Midfielder

D.O.B.
18.10.94

Birthplace
Glasgow

Previous Club
Hibernian

Date Signed
August 2018

Trezeguet
Midfielder

D.O.B.
01.10.94

Birthplace
Kafr el Sheikh, Egypt

Previous Club
Kasimpasa

Date Signed
July 2019

Jota
Forward

D.O.B.
16.06.91

Birthplace
A Pobra do Caraminal, Spain

Previous Club
Birmingham

Date Signed
June 2019

Keinan Davis
Forward

D.O.B.
13.02.98

Birthplace
Stevenage

Previous Club
Biggleswade Town

Date Signed
December 2015

Scott Hogan
Forward

D.O.B.
13.04.92

Birthplace
Salford

Previous Club
Brentford

Date Signed
January 2017

Callum O'Hare
Midfielder

D.O.B.
01.05.98

Birthplace
Solihull

Previous Club
N/A

Date Signed
Academy Graduate

Jonathan Kodjia
Forward

D.O.B.
22.10.89

Birthplace
Paris, France

Previous Club
Bristol City

Date Signed
August 2016

Wesley Moraes
Forward

D.O.B.
26.11.96

Birthplace
Juiz de Fora, Brazil

Previous Club
Club Brugge

Date Signed
July 2019

TYRONE
MINGS

AUTOGRAPH

IS THIS THE
LIBRARY?

As you might expect for a club of this stature, dozens of books have been written about Villa.

Apart from autobiographies by star names like Brian Little, Paul McGrath and Peter Withe, there have also been numerous books tracing the club's exploits in the FA Cup, League Cup and European competitions.

Here's a small selection of the publications which have graced the shelves of book stores and libraries down the years.

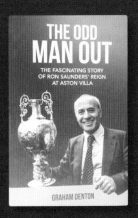

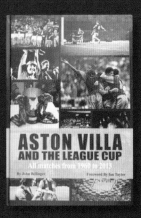

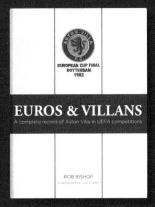

WHERE IT ALL STARTED

Can you match these Villa players with the clubs where they began their professional careers?

1 JED STEER

2 NEIL TAYLOR

3 JOHN McGINN

4 TYRONE MINGS

5 JOTA

6 ANWAR EL GHAZI

7 CONOR HOURIHANE

8 JACK GREALISH

9 JONATHAN KODJIA

10 FREDERIC GUILBERT

A IPSWICH TOWN ▶ 4

B NORWICH CITY ▶

C REIMS ▶

D ASTON VILLA ▶

E CHERBOURG ▶

F AJAX ▶

G CELTA VIGO ▶

H SUNDERLAND ▶

I ST. MIRREN ▶

J WREXHAM ▶

Answers on Page 60

26

MATT
TARGETT

AVFC

AUTOGRAPH

GREAT SCOTS

John McGinn is the latest in a long line of great Scottish players to have represented Villa down the years. With the help of his name, and the clues below, can you name 10 other great Scots?

Answers on Page 60

The crossword grid spells vertically: **J O H N M C G I N N**

1. **First name of Cowan**, a commanding defender who played 356 games for Villa in the late 19th and early 20th centuries.

2. **Ian R** ... Former Liverpool player who was Villa's first captain in European competition.

3. **Ray H** ... A Republic of Ireland international who was born in Glasgow.

4. **Des B** ... Busy midfielder who helped Villa to win the League Championship and European Cup.

5. **Bobby T** ... Prolific striker who scored 70 goals and helped Villa to their first League Cup triumph in 1961.

6. **Alan Mc** ... Late 1980s striker who was known as Rambo.

7. **Andy G** ... One of the bravest strikers ever to play for Villa, he signed from Dundee United in 1975.

8. **Charlie A** ... Classy left-back who holds the club's appearance record with 660 games.

9. **Allan E** ... Signed as a striker, he was transformed into a defender, helping Villa to glory in the early 1980s.

10. **Ken Mc** ... Allan's central defensive partner in the Championship and European Cup-winning teams.

PROUD TO WEAR THE SHIRT

But whose is it? Can you unravel these anagrams to reveal the players' names?

HIS LAGER

1

AJOT

2

LUGER BIT

3

GI HAZEL

4

OK SAN

5

TERSE

6

HOLD ME A YAM

7

M SING

8

LAY ROT

9

HER SECT

10

EU ASH

11

HER? NAH! IOU!

12

Answers on Page 60

HELP CHIP OUT OF THE MAZE

Can you help Chip get out of the maze and join Bella and the Villa fans

Answer on Page 61

JOTA

AUTOGRAPH

SEEING THE
LIGHT!

Floodlights are an integral part of football, but that wasn't always the case.

Until the early 1950s, teams had to kick off at 2.00pm on Saturdays during the winter months, while evening matches were unheard of.

But everything changed with the introduction of floodlighting. Villa Park's first system was installed in the summer of 1958 and comprised 180-foot tall pylons in all four corners of the ground, each one holding 48 150-watt lamps.

The lights were switched on at half-time in a match against Portsmouth on Monday 25th August 1958, and Johnny Dixon was the first player to score under them.

In 1970, the installation of powerful new lamps enabled Villa to be the first club to stage a televised match in colour – an FA Cup semi-final between Leeds United and Manchester United.

The following year saw the introduction of the iconic lamp formation which saw the corners of Villa Park lit up by the letters A and V – and these remained until the pylons began to be dismantled in 1989.

Since then, the stadium has been illuminated by lights located along the roof of the stands.

2018/19

SEASON
REVIEW

AUGUST

Villa get off to a flying start, kicking off the season with back-to-back victories for the first time since 1999.

Steve Bruce's men open the new campaign with a 3-1 win at Hull City, where Tommy Elphick and Ahmed Elmohamady both score their first goals for the club before Alan Hutton seals victory with a low shot into the corner of the net.

Birkir Bjarnason's stoppage-time effort ensures a dramatic 3-2 victory over Wigan Athletic in the opening home game but Villa then have to settle for three consecutive Championship draws, against Ipswich Town, Brentford and Reading.

A Conor Hourihane goal ensures a 1-0 Carabao Cup win at Yeovil before Villa go out by the same score at Burton Albion in the second round.

SEPTEMBER

Anwar El Ghazi's first goal for the club is only a consolation as Villa's unbeaten Championship start comes to a halt in a 4-1 defeat by Sheffield United at Bramall Lane.

Conor Hourihane's last-gasp free-kick earns a 1-1 draw against Blackburn Rovers at Ewood Park before loan signings Tammy Abraham and Yannick Bolasie mark their home debuts by scoring in a 2-0 victory over Rotherham United.

John McGinn's spectacular volley against Sheffield Wednesday isn't enough to prevent Villa's first home defeat of the season, although Birkir Bjarnason's header on the stroke of half-time earns a 1-1 draw against Bristol City at Ashton Gate.

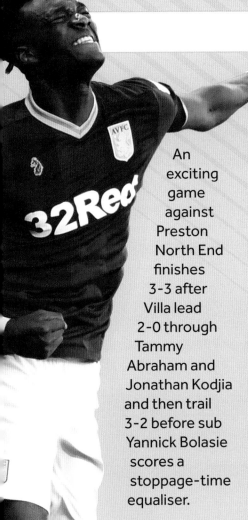

OCTOBER

An exciting game against Preston North End finishes 3-3 after Villa lead 2-0 through Tammy Abraham and Jonathan Kodjia and then trail 3-2 before sub Yannick Bolasie scores a stoppage-time equaliser.

Even then, there's still time for a winner but Glenn Whelan's weak penalty is saved, costing Villa two points and Steve Bruce his job.

Lifelong Villa supporter Dean Smith is appointed the club's head coach and gets off to a flying start as Abraham's early goal – his third in as many games – clinches a 1-0 win over Swansea City.

Sadly, Smith's first two away games are less successful as Villa slip to defeats by Norwich City and QPR in the space of four days.

NOVEMBER

Villa fans witness some remarkable performances during November. After a home win over struggling Bolton Wanderers, the team produce a stylish performance at Pride Park to beat Derby County 3-0 with late goals from John McGinn, Tammy Abraham and Conor Hourihane.

That's followed by an exhilarating Second City derby in which Birmingham City take the lead before Dean Smith's side storm ahead through Jonathan Kodjia, Jack Grealish and an Abraham penalty. Although our neighbours reduce the deficit, victory is sealed by a sensational solo goal from Alan Hutton.

After three straight wins, Villa manage only a point against Nottingham Forest, but the 5-5 draw is one of the most breath-taking games ever seen at Villa Park.

Villa trail three times and then lead 5-4 before the visitors grab a late equaliser. Abraham scores four of our goals – the first Villa player to hit four in one game since 1988.

DECEMBER

Villa turn on the style for an emphatic 3-0 win against Middlesbrough at The Riverside before experiencing fluctuating fortunes in back-to-back 2-2 draws.

Leading twice through Anwar El Ghazi goals against West Bromwich Albion, they are left frustrated at The Hawthorns when Jay Rodriguez appears to handle the ball as he scoops it over the line for a late equaliser.

Villa then trail twice at home to Stoke City but hit back on each occasion, first with a Tammy Abraham penalty and then a header from Jonathan Kodjia.

Abraham and Conor Hourihane establish a two-goal lead against high-riding Leeds United, only for the visitors to draw level and then snatch a stoppage-time winner.

Hourihane's 65th-minute header secures a 1-0 win at Swansea on Boxing Day before Abraham's 14th goal in 19 Villa games earns a 1-1 draw at Preston.

JANUARY

There's relief all around Villa Park after rumours that Tammy Abraham is joining Wolves during the transfer window prove to be unfounded.

The lad simply can't stop scoring, hitting five goals in January to take his Villa total to 19 in 23 Championship games since arriving on loan from Chelsea.

Abraham both starts and ends the month by netting twice in one game.

His brace earns a point against Queens Park Rangers on New Year's Day, and he is also on target twice – including a penalty – in a 2-1 victory over Ipswich Town.

The young striker's other goal salvages a point after Villa trail 2-0 at home to Hull City, James Chester's powerful header having reduced the deficit just before half-time.

FEBRUARY

After dominating but failing to make a breakthrough in a goalless draw at Reading, Villa are involved in an amazing Friday night home game against Sheffield United.

Trailing 3-0 to a Billy Sharp hat-trick with just nine minutes remaining, Dean Smith's men battle their way back with a header from new boy Tyrone Mings and a tap-in from Tammy Abraham before substitute Andre Green heads a stoppage-time equaliser to complete a dramatic finale.

A late Neal Maupay goal leaves Villa pointless at Brentford before neighbours West Bromwich Albion put another dent in our play-off prospects by winning 2-0 at Villa Park with two goals in four minutes from Hal Robson-Kanu and Jay Rodriguez.

A third straight defeat is averted when Albert Adomah fires home his first goal of the season to cancel out Sam Vokes's early breakthrough for Stoke City.

JANUARY RESULTS

JAN 1
Q.P.R. (H)   2-2
Abraham 2

JAN 5
SWANSEA (FAC 3) (H)   0-3

JAN 12
WIGAN ATHLETIC (A)   0-3

JAN 19
HULL CITY (H)   2-2
Chester, Abraham

JAN 26
IPSWICH TOWN (H)   2-1
Abraham 2 (1 pen)

FEBRUARY RESULTS

FEB 2
READING (A)   0-0

FEB 8
SHEFFIELD UTD (H)   3-3
Mings, Abraham, Green

FEB 13
BRENTFORD (A)   0-1

FEB 16
WEST BROM. (H)   0-2

FEB 23
STOKE CITY (A)   1-1
Adomah

MARCH

What a sensational return to action for Jack Grealish! Ruled out for three months by a knee injury, Grealish is appointed captain on his return to the team for the home match against Derby County.

His impact couldn't be any more significant, Villa racing into a 4-0 lead by half-time. Conor Hourihane is on target twice, either side of Tammy Abraham's 21st goal for the club before Grealish crowns a superb display with a sensational 20-yard volley from Glenn Whelan's corner.

Grealish follows up by hitting the only goal in the Second City derby at St Andrew's before John McGinn scores twice in a 3-1 win at Nottingham Forest, Kortney Hause securing all three points with his first goal for the club.

A vibrant performance produces a comfortable home win over Middlesbrough, thanks to Anwar El Ghazi, John McGinn and sub Albert Adomah, before Villa sign off a successful month by beating Blackburn Rovers.

Goals from Abraham and Tyrone Mings make it five consecutive wins during March – a feat never previously achieved in the club's 145-year history.

Villa just can't stop winning as they extend their sequence of consecutive league victories to a record-breaking 10 games.

The match against Sheffield Wednesday at Hillsborough is heading for a draw after John McGinn's equaliser leaves the score at 1-1 going into stoppage time. But a dramatic finale sees Albert Adomah put them in front before Tammy Abraham completes a 3-1 victory.

Trailing again at Rotherham, Dean Smith's men hit back with a Jonathan Kodjia penalty and a Jack Grealish goal just after half-time to seal a 2-1 win – and it's the same outcome the following Saturday, when Abraham (penalty) and Conor Hourihane are the men on target against Bristol City at Villa Park.

That's followed by a very happy Easter. A 2-0 Good Friday success at Bolton, courtesy of second-half headers from Grealish and Abraham, is followed on Easter Monday by Jonathan Kodjia's first-half winner against Millwall.

The winning run ends with a 1-1 draw against Leeds United at Elland Road, where the home side sportingly allow sub Albert Adomah to equalise immediately after taking the lead with a controversial goal.

THE PLAY-OFFS

Wembley wonders!

There's nothing like winning on English football's greatest stage – and Villa made it a day to remember when they beat Derby County at Wembley to secure their return to the Premier League.

A 2-1 victory over the Rams in the Championship play-off final more than made amends for the disappointment of 12 months earlier when we were beaten by Fulham at the national stadium.

This time it was delight all the way as goals from Anwar El Ghazi and John McGinn sparked scenes of jubilation at the final whistle.

The players raced to the west stand to salute the claret-and-blue faithful for their amazing support, Prince William couldn't hide his emotion as he embraced Villa's former Norwegian striker John Carew – and Villa-related songs boomed out over the PA system.

In the play-off semi-final, Dean Smith's side needed a penalty shoot-out to overcome neighbours West Bromwich Albion after the tie finished 2-2 on aggregate.

Jed Steer was the hero in the shoot-out at The Hawthorns, saving Albion's first two kicks before Villa emerged 4-3 winners with conversions by Conor Hourihane, Mile Jedinak, Jack Grealish and Tammy Abraham.

PLAY-OFF SEMI-FINAL

MAY 11 - 1ST LEG
WEST BROM (H)   **2-1**
Hourihane, Abraham (pen)

MAY 15 - 2ND LEG
WEST BROM (A)   **0-1**
Agg 2-2
Villa win 4-3 on penalties

PLAY-OFF FINAL

MAY 27
DERBY (N)   **2-1**
El Ghazi, McGinn

DEBUT DAY

It's always a special occasion when a footballer makes his debut for a new club – particularly when he is playing for Villa!

Eleven players experienced the thrill throughout the course of the 2018-19 campaign, and although some of them were not even at the club at the end of the season, we're sure they will always remember their big day in a Villa shirt.

JOHN McGINN	Wigan Athletic (H)	3-2
ORJAN NYLAND	Wigan Athletic (H)	3-2
ANDRE MOREIRA	Yeovil (A)	1-0
ANWAR EL GHAZI	Reading (H)	1-1
TAMMY ABRAHAM	Blackburn Rovers (A)	1-1
YANNICK BOLASIE	Blackburn Rovers (A)	1-1
LOVRE KALINIC	Swansea City (H)	0-3
KORTNEY HAUSE	Wigan Athletic (A)	0-3
TYRONE MINGS	Reading (A)	0-0
TOM CARROLL	Reading (A)	0-0
JACOB RAMSEY	West Brom. (H)	0-2

TREZEGUET

AUTOGRAPH

VILLANS
IN A SPIN

Modern-day viewing and audio are all about downloading and streaming.

But for many enthusiasts, there's nothing to beat owning "hard copies" of films or music – particularly when they feature your favourite football club.

Over the years, Villa have appeared frequently on various recording formats, including vinyl, cassette, CD, VHS and DVD.

Here's a selection of releases which have featured match action, interviews and songs about the boys in claret and blue – including one which claims Father Christmas is a Villa fan!

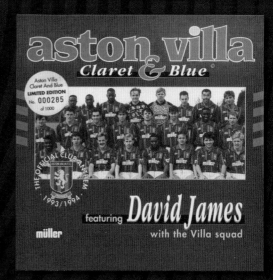

YEAR OF RELEASE: 1971

FORMAT: VINYL LP

YEAR OF RELEASE: 1994

FORMAT: VINYL 7-INCH SINGLE

YEAR OF RELEASE: 1981

FORMAT: VINYL LP

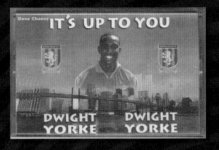

YEAR OF RELEASE: 1996

FORMAT: CASSETTE

YEAR OF RELEASE: 1994

FORMAT: VHS VIDEO

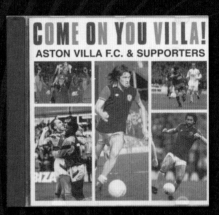

YEAR OF RELEASE: 1996

FORMAT: CD

YEAR OF RELEASE: 2003

FORMAT: CD SINGLE

YEAR OF RELEASE: 2007

FORMAT: DVD

EZRI
KONSA

AUTOGRAPH

FUNNY FACES

Each of the funny faces below are made up
of three Villa players, can you name each player?

If you need a clue the nine players can also be
found in the wordsearch at the bottom of the page.

1		1		1
2		2		2
3		3		3

C	W	E	S	L	E	Y	A	N	M	T
W	O	P	Y	O	M	X	N	G	C	R
J	R	T	M	L	O	I	B	R	G	E
H	O	U	R	I	H	A	N	E	I	Z
T	H	T	S	E	N	N	S	G	N	E
G	R	E	A	L	I	S	H	A	S	G
N	T	B	S	G	W	E	S	L	E	U
Q	A	O	C	D	Q	M	L	E	Y	E
E	L	M	O	H	A	M	A	D	Y	T
E	D	U	J	S	T	E	E	R	G	F

Answers on page 61

PART of the PRIDE

Following Villa is a lifetime experience – and you can start as early as you like!

Young supporters are vital to the club, which is why we offer so many great benefits to members of our brilliant junior section, The Cubs.

One of Villa's most important aims is to welcome families and bring young fans closer to the club – we're very much a Pride of Lions!

That's where The Cubs comes in. Membership is FREE to all junior season ticket holders and offers members some great benefits throughout the year.

These include:

- A welcome pack, including an exclusive pin badge just for members and a very special gift that you won't find anywhere else!
- Exclusive competitions.
- Invites to the increasingly popular Christmas party with the opportunity to meet first-team players.
- A birthday and Christmas card.
- You will also be enrolled into the new Villa Pride Rewards scheme, with loads of competitions offering once-in-a-lifetime prizes.

There are also plenty of other opportunities to be closer to the club. Mascots Hercules, Bella and Chip will also be on hand at the many other events held at Villa Park, with a firm focus on welcoming new families.

This is epitomised by the regular Family Fun Zone on match days, an area which continues to grow and improve with the help of supporters' feedback.

And even for those youngsters who are not junior season ticket holders, the cost for all of this is just £20 a year! To enroll just call 0333 323 1874 or go to www.avfc.co.uk/membership

EURO NUMBERS

4 Villa have converted four penalties in European ties, **Gareth Barry** netting two of them against Celta Vigo (2000) and Litex Lovech (2008). The others were scored by Stan Collymore (v Celta Vigo, 1998) and James Milner (v Rapid Vienna, 2009).

9 **Gary Shaw** and Peter Withe are the club's highest scorers in UEFA competitions with nine goals each. They are also two of the three players to have scored a hat-trick for Villa in European ties, along with Stan Collymore.

24 Apart from home games at Villa Park (and The Hawthorns), Villa have played European ties in 24 countries: Belgium, Turkey, Poland, Spain, Iceland, East Germany, Ukraine, Holland, Romania, Italy, Portugal, Russia, Czechoslovakia, Slovakia, Czech Republic, Sweden, France, Norway, Croatia, Switzerland, Denmark, Bulgaria, Germany and Austria.

5 Five of **Ken McNaught**'s 13 Villa goals were scored in European ties – all of them headers. The Scottish defender was on target twice against Gornik Zabrze in 1977 and also scored against Barcelona in the UEFA Cup (1978), Dynamo Kiev in the European Cup (1982) and Barcelona again in the 1983 UEFA Super Cup.

29 The highest number of games played by a Villa player in European games. The figure was achieved by two midfielders – **Gordon Cowans** and Dennis Mortimer.

50 The highest number shirt worn by a Villa player in European competition. Midfielder Jonathan Hogg wore No 50 in the first leg of the Europa League play-off against Rapid Vienna in August 2010.

125 The number of Villa goals in European ties between 1975 and 2010.

167 The official attendance for the first round European Cup clash against Besiktas in September 1982. The game was played behind closed doors at Villa Park following crowd disturbances at the previous season's semi-final against Anderlecht in Brussels. The only people allowed inside the stadium were the police, the press, club officials and Villa staff members.

49,619 The highest attendance for a European tie at Villa Park was 49,619 for the first leg of the UEFA Cup quarter-final against Barcelona in 1978.

1982 The best number of them all! On 26th May 1982, Villa became champions of Europe, beating Bayern Munich 1-0 in the final. Captain Dennis Mortimer proudly held aloft the European Cup after Peter Withe's 67th-minute goal proved enough to beat the mighty German outfit. The skipper and the striker are pictured with manager Tony Barton, showing the trophy to Villa's jubilant fans.

10/10

It's a record for the Villa class of 2019

Breaking football records isn't easy, particularly when a record has stood for over a century!

But Villa's Class of 2019 did it when they reeled off ten consecutive league wins in March and April – one more than the figure achieved by their claret-and-blue counterparts in 1910.

No-one could have imagined that club history was about to be made when Villa slipped into the bottom half of the Championship table in February.

But the players responded with an incredible run of results which carried them to the play-offs.

It all started on the day Jack Grealish returned from injury and was appointed captain. Villa won 4-0 against Derby – Super Jack scoring with a stunning volley.

And it just got better and better as Dean Smith's men followed up with wins over Birmingham City, Nottingham Forest, Middlesbrough, Blackburn Rovers, Sheffield Wednesday, Rotherham United, Bristol City, Bolton Wanderers and Millwall.

Here are a few memorable images from that record-breaking run...

54

vs Middlesbrough

vs Sheffield Wed.

vs Blackburn

vs Rotherham

vs Bolton

vs Millwall

BADGES OF HONOUR

Villa fans collect all sorts of memorabilia, and enamel badges are proving increasingly popular with supporters of all ages.

Some of them are quite valuable, too, so we can only imagine the value of the thousand or so badges on this blazer!

Holte Ender Ben Costello inherited the amazing collection from his father, who worked for Villa for nearly 30 years in various capacities.

He uses a match-day blazer to exhibit the vast collection, which is covered both front and back with Villa badges from all around the world.

There are numerous limited editions, including one of just 25 produced for our visit to White Hart Lane for Tottenham's 125th anniversary game in 2007.

As you can see, badges are produced for all sorts of reasons, and some even feature Disney characters such as Mickey Mouse and Snow White and the Seven Dwarfs!

WESLEY
MORAES

AUTOGRAPH

Record Transfers

Before the summer of 2019, Villa's record signing was striker Darren Bent, who cost £18million from Sunderland in 2011.

It was by far the biggest fee Villa had ever paid for a new player – one and a half times the £12m paid for James Milner in 2008.

Even so, it was money well spent, Bent scoring nine goals by the end of the season to ensure that Villa stayed in the Premier League.

But what about our other record signings down the years? Well, the first "big money" signing made by Villa was a player called Archie Goodall, who cost the princely sum of £100!

Goodall arrived from Preston in October 1888 – the first year of the Football League – and he was such a versatile footballer that he played in five different positions. He scored seven goals in 14 games before leaving to join Derby County the following season.

Since those early days, the club's transfer record has been broken 33 times, and the list on the opposite page outlines all of Villa's record buys before Wesley's arrival.

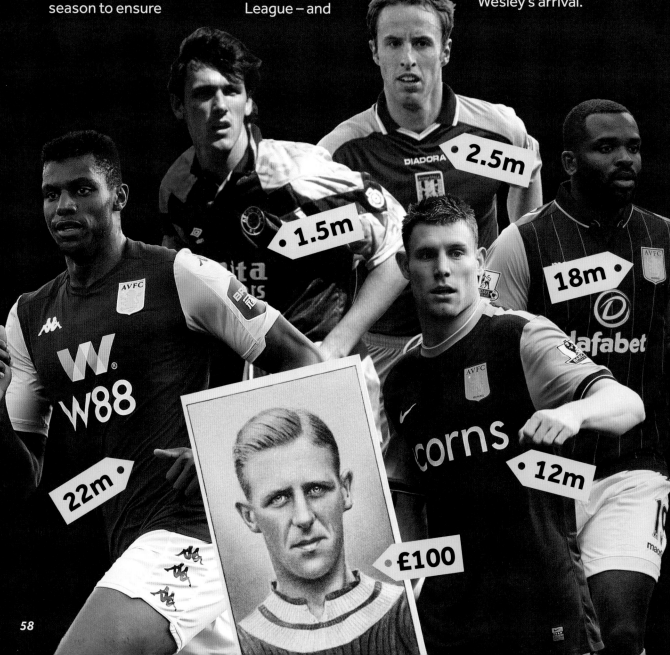

58

Date	Player	Previous club	Fee (£)
Jan 2011	**DARREN BENT**	Sunderland	18m
Aug 2008	**JAMES MILNER**	Newcastle United	12m
Jan 2007	**ASHLEY YOUNG**	Watford	9.6m
Jan 2001	**JUAN PABLO ANGEL**	River Plate	9.5m
May 1997	**STAN COLLYMORE**	Liverpool	7m
Aug 1996	**SASA CURCIC**	Bolton Wanderers	4m
July 1995	**SAVO MILOSEVIC**	Partizan Belgrade	3.5m
July 1995	**GARETH SOUTHGATE**	Crystal Palace	2.5m
Sept 1993	**DEAN SAUNDERS**	Liverpool	2.3m
Feb 1992	**EARL BARRETT**	Oldham Athletic	1.7m
July 1991	**DALIAN ATKINSON**	Real Sociedad	1.6m
Mar 1990	**TONY CASCARINO**	Millwall	1.5m
Feb 1989	**IAN ORMONDROYD**	Bradford City	650,000
May 1980	**PETER WITHE**	Newcastle Utd	500,000
Sept 1979	**DAVID GEDDIS**	Ipswich Town	300,000
Jan 1978	**TOMMY CRAIG**	Newcastle Utd	270,000
Aug 1977	**KEN McNAUGHT**	Everton	200,000
Dec 1975	**DENNIS MORTIMER**	Coventry City	175,000
Sept 1975	**ANDY GRAY**	Dundee United	110,000
July 1969	**BRUCE RIOCH**	Luton Town	100,000
Sept 1968	**BARRIE HOLE**	Blackburn Rovers	65,000
May 1968	**MIKE FERGUSON**	Blackburn Rovers	55,000
Sept 1964	**JOHNNY MacLEOD**	Arsenal	40,000
Dec 1950	**DAVE WALSH**	West Brom	25,000
Dec 1948	**IVOR POWELL**	QPR	17,500
Jan 1947	**TREVOR FORD**	Swansea Town	12,000
June 1934	**JIMMY ALLEN**	Portsmouth	10,775
April 1927	**JIMMY GIBSON**	Partick Thistle	7,500
Oct 1919	**FRANK BARSON**	Barnsley	2,850
June 1912	**ANDY DUCAT**	Woolwich Arsenal	1,000
May 1907	**CHARLIE WALLACE**	Crystal Palace	500
Aug 1895	**JIMMY CRABTREE**	Burnley	250
Oct 1888	**ARCHIE GOODALL**	Preston North End	100

QUIZ ANSWERS

DO YOU KNOW? JACK GREALISH
(PAGE 15)

1. MANCHESTER CITY
2. LEICESTER CITY
3. REPUBLIC OF IRELAND
4. FOUR (the 2015 FA Cup semi-final and final, and the 2018 and 2019 Championship play-off finals)
5. DERBY COUNTY
6. ASTON VILLA – WHO ELSE?!!!

WHERE IT ALL STARTED
(PAGE 26)

1 – B   (Jed Steer/Norwich City)
2 – J   (Neil Taylor/Wrexham)
3 – I   (John McGinn/St Mirren)
4 – A   (Tyrone Mings/Ipswich Town)
5 – G   (Jota/Celta Vigo)
6 – F   (Anwar El Ghazi/Ajax)
7 – H   (Conor Hourihane/Sunderland)
8 – D   (Jack Grealish/Villa)
9 – C   (Jonathan Kodjia/Reims)
10 – E (Frederic Guilbert/Cherbourg)

GREAT SCOTS
(PAGE 28)

				J	A	M	E	S		
			R	O	S	S				
	H	O	U	G	H	T	O	N		
	B	R	E	M	N	E	R			
	T	H	O	M	S	O	N			
		M	C	I	N	A	L	L	Y	
		G	R	A	Y					
		A	I	T	K	E	N			
E	V	A	N	S						
	M	C	N	A	U	G	H	T		

PROUD TO WEAR THE SHIRT (PAGE 29)

1   GREALISH
2   JOTA
3   GUILBERT
4   EL GHAZI
5   KONSA
6   STEER
7   ELMOHAMADY
8   MINGS
9   TAYLOR
10 CHESTER
11 HAUSE
12 HOURIHANE

CHIP'S MAZE
(PAGE 30)

FUNNY FACES
(PAGE 49)

FACE 1

STEER
HOURIHANE
TREZEGUET

FACE 2

ELMOHAMADY
MINGS
WESLEY

FACE 3

GREALISH
MCGINN
JOTA

C	W	E	S	L	E	Y	A	N	M	T
W	O	P	Y	O	M	X	N	G	C	R
J	R	T	M	L	O	I	B	R	G	E
H	O	U	R	I	H	A	N	E	I	Z
T	H	T	S	E	N	N	S	G	N	E
G	R	E	A	L	I	S	H	A	S	G
N	T	B	S	G	W	E	S	L	E	U
Q	A	O	C	D	Q	M	L	E	Y	E
E	L	M	O	H	A	M	A	D	Y	T
E	D	U	J	S	T	E	E	R	G	F

FACE 1

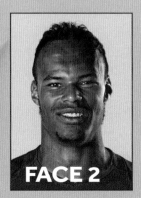

FACE 2

FACE 3

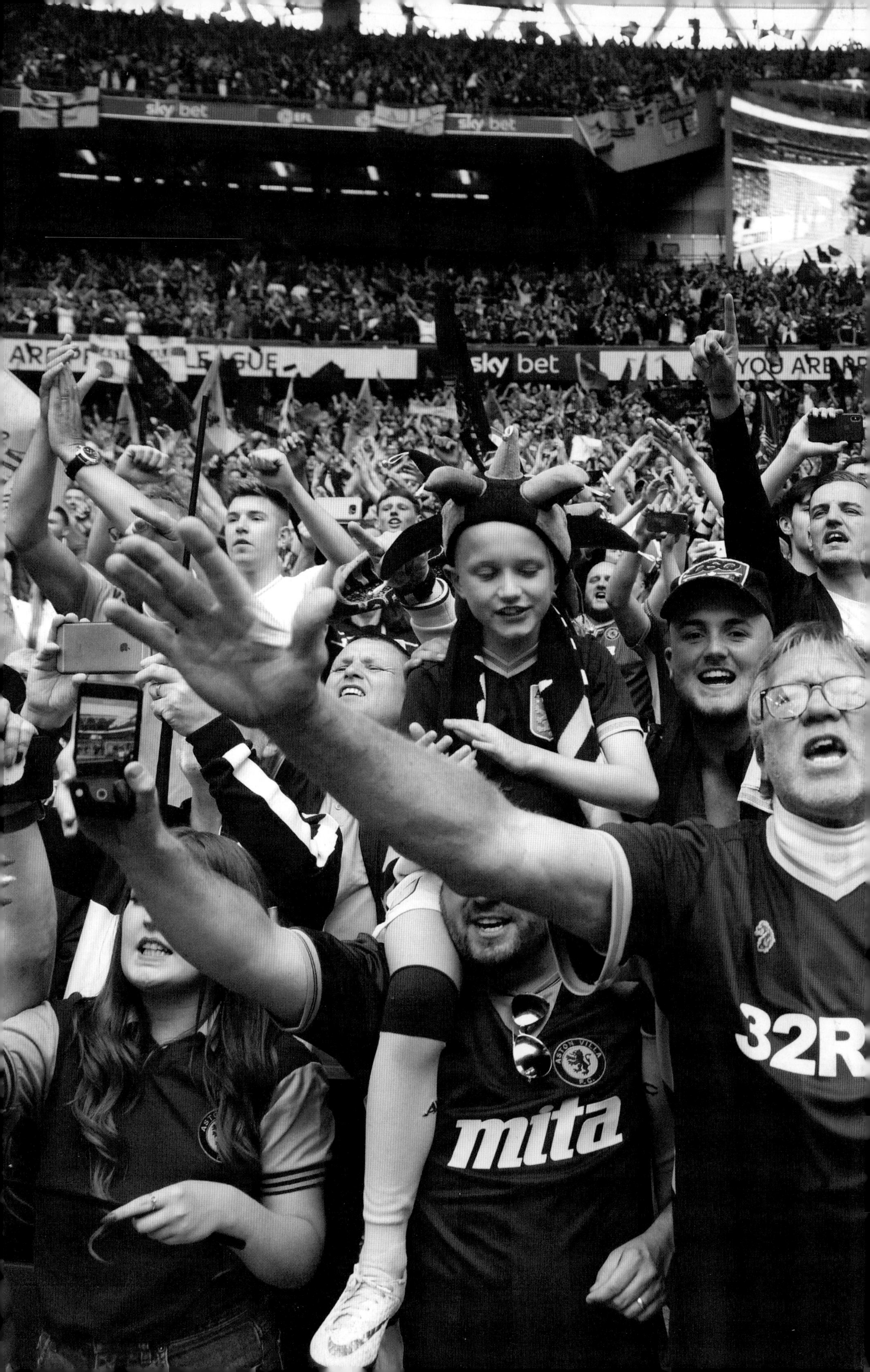
sky bet
sky bet
sky bet
ASTON VILLA F.C.
mita